Music is for all children . . . four and five year olds as well as grade schoolers . . . children labeled as "nonmusical" and those considered gifted. . . .

So Connie Fortunato, director of a graded choir program for children and an experienced classroom music teacher, suggests a new approach.

No longer should children be required to sit still and memorize songs by rote. They can *experience* music . . . they can imitate a rhythmic phrase by stamping to a grandoise march . . . they can jump from a line to a space on a large staff that has been masking-taped to the floor . . . they can learn by doing, feeling, enjoying.

And if we adults choose the music carefully and thoughtfully . . . children can learn and retain Christian truth more firmly than most of us dreamed.

MUSIC IS FOR CHILDREN will convince you that music is not just a frill or a time filler . . . it's one of God's beautiful avenues for enriching all our lives.

MUSIC IS FOR CHILDREN

Connie Fortunato

David C. Cook Publishing Co.

ELGIN, ILLINOIS—WESTON, ONTARIO
FULLERTON, CALIFORNIA

Credit and appreciation are due publishers and copyright owners for the use of the following:

"I Am a Promise" © Copyright 1975 by William J. Gaither. International copyright secured. All rights reserved. Printed in the U.S.A. Used by special permission of the publisher.

"It's Not Easy Being Green" Words and Music by Joe Raposo. © 1970 and 1972. Jonico Music, Inc. All rights reserved.

"I Wonder How It Felt" © Copyright 1974 by William J. Gaither. International copyright secured. All rights reserved. Printed in the U.S.A. Used by special permission of the publisher.

"Oh, How He Loves you and Me" © 1975 Word Music, Inc. All rights reserved. Used by permission.

MUSIC IS FOR CHILDREN

Published by David C. Cook Publishing Co., Elgin, IL 60120
Edited by Janet Hoover Thoma

Printed in the United States of America
Library of Congress Catalog Number: 78-50962
ISBN: 0-89191-128-6

To my husband, Jim, without whose encouragement
I would have never completed this task

and

To my children, Stephanie and Stephen, whose lives
sparked the idea and gave me the impetus.

CONTENTS

EVERYONE CAN!

"C'MON, YOU CAN DO IT!" How many times has that kind of pressure roped you into a situation that surprisingly turned out to be fun? With the lure of success dangling in front of you, you abandoned your fears and took the plunge.

All of us thrive on success. We like to do things that display our achievements. We avoid activities that make us look clumsy, dumb, or inept.

Our interest in music reflects this desire for competence. If our natural ability has been encouraged in earlier years, we enjoy listening to a Bach concerto or singing in the church choir. If not, we veer away from such involvement. But as children, most of us *would* have been able to express ourselves musically.

I'll never forget driving home one morning after taking my little girl to kindergarten. My two-year-old son was sitting in the back in his car seat. All of a sudden, I heard a beautiful, note-perfect tune.

"Mother, I love you / How much I love you / I just want you to see / God gave you to me."

I was flabbergasted! Not only had the song incited all kinds of warm mother's pride; my son had sung an intricate melodic and rhythmic pattern.

Let me skip back a few more years—this time to a cozy kitchen in Hanover Park, Illinois. It was a bright, sunny morning, and eighteen-month-old Stephanie was in her playpen. I'd just returned from Saturday music classes, which I taught to four- and five-year-old children. In my exuberance to be home, I walked into the kitchen, clapped three times, and then paused.

Stephanie's eyes widened with excitement. I clapped again as I said, "One, two, three, rest."

Stephanie looked at me with a sparkle that only a toddler can muster and clapped, *one, two, three,* and paused.

Now don't scrap these as isolated instances. My children are no more "musically inclined" than much of the young population. Music and rhythm can be learned by the young child, because the child's ear for sound is still developing and, therefore, is very receptive.

MUSIC IS A LANGUAGE

An example of this is a child's facility with language. It has been said that if we waited to expose children to their native language until the age of eight, they would never learn to speak. Children born in foreign countries speak a second language without the slightest accent, while their parents, regardless of their proficiency, will always sound like foreigners. Certainly the difference between the children and their parents does not lie in their ability to understand the syntax or to produce the sounds. The difference is in the ear!

The scientific community—doctors, developmental psychologists, and educators—have established that 70 percent of the human ear develops between the ages of three and seven. Another new discovery makes this even more exciting: sounds that become native to the ear during these years will not be erased by subsequent experience. If children who learn to speak without an accent are removed from a culture and return later, they will have lost none of their perfect accent.

What does all this have to do with music?

Music is a language, too. It is capable of communicating substance as well as feeling, atmosphere, and emotion. And music is made up of many intricate parts. There may or may not be words, which convey a certain message. But there is always a tone or melody. This is what catches you and repeats itself in your head throughout the day.

Harmony provides the supporting structure for that tune. It adds the dimension of depth. And rhythm is the heartbeat or pulse, recurring with such precision that before long you're tapping your foot or wiggling your finger in time to the music.

Timbre is the personality of sound. It distinguishes the sound of a trumpet from the sound of a violin or piano. Finally, there is the aspect of pitch. Although this involves the vibrations of sound per second, we all recognize poor pitch when we hear a sour note.

The amazing thing about music is that an intellectual

understanding of each of these parts—or any of them—is not needed to enjoy it. Enjoyment comes through the ear, not from a successful diagnosis of the harmony or rhythm.

Get a bunch of kids together and put on a Sesame Street record. Even if they have never watched the TV program or learned any of its songs, it won't be long before they are tapping or beating to the rhythm, singing the tune, or moving their body in response to the feelings they get from listening.

THE "MUSICAL" CHILD

In my years of teaching music to young children, some parents have told me that their child showed musical initiative or interest. Other parents have enrolled their "not particularly musical" child because they wanted to expose the child to music.

Theoretically, I should have had both "musical" and "nonmusical" children in my classes. But these children have consistently demonstrated almost *equal ability*. Allowing for natural differences in personality, the child who has been tagged as nonmusical may end up at the head of the class.

Our definition of the word *musical* is responsible for such labeling. For years a child who could sing a tune at an early age or pick one out on the piano was considered a musical genius. While this may be true, the converse is not. Just because a child does not go to the piano and play "Mary Had a Little Lamb" or sing "Yankee Doodle" at age three does not mean he is a musical dud. Many times children don't have a piano at home or parents who play records or encourage them to sing.

I remember when I first introduced music instruction

into the regular Sunday school time. I am sure that many adults questioned my purpose. Why, these children hadn't been screened—some of them couldn't even "carry a tune." How could I ever combine "musical" and "nonmusical" children in the same experience? And why during Sunday school?

Within a few short weeks, children who had been shy and unwilling to participate became eager to be involved. All of the children could recite more Scripture verses than they had learned in the previous three years. And many of them were singing some of the songs during the week to their families.

For the first time ever, moms and dads knew what their children had been learning in Sunday school instead of the traditional "What did you learn today?" And the shrugged reply, "Nothing."

Because we are beginning to recognize a child's natural ability, music education for young children has mushroomed in the last twenty years. Prior to that time, most music instructors would not accept children until age seven or eight. Any child who started younger and achieved a degree of success was considered to be a prodigy. It was thought that a child needed to read and understand the basic concepts of arithmetic to learn music successfully.

Then some innovators began to contend that music should be learned in much the same way as language—through the ear. If a child could master a language by the age of five, and music could be taught by a similar process, music education was not only possible for the young child, it was most easily achieved then.

This premise has revolutionized music instruction all over the world. Five leading methods are now prominent, but they all share a common foundation: music should be learned through the ear and thus should be *experienced* first.

What do we mean by experiencing? Go back with me to Stephanie in her playpen. She had not listened to a mathematical explanation of quarter notes and a quarter rest. She had simply heard *clap, clap, clap, pause.* Her response showed that she had experienced that rhythm.

Musical concepts can be learned by having children experience them. For instance, let's take the concept of high and low, which children associate with volume because of parental conditioning. (How often have you said, "That TV is up too high. Turn it down"?)

It is easy to see that some redefinition is necessary. Rather than simply describing what high and low notes are, you might speak to the children in a quiet but very high voice. Stretch your arms up as high as they will go, then stand on your tiptoes and reach for the sky. In your high-pitched voice, talk about the birds singing and flying in the sky.

Now swoop your hands down to the floor as your voice drops to its lowest possible pitch. As you play this game—all the time keeping your voice at the same volume—you will notice that the children begin to experience the difference in pitch.

Then slip to the piano and replace those high-pitched vocal tones with high sounds on the piano. Now use a big glissando sweep down to the bass notes. Often the children will automatically respond by bending over as far as they can to touch the floor. You may want to call the low tones "elephants" and the high tones "birds." Whatever you choose, you have involved the children in experiencing the difference between high and low. Before you know it, they will distinguish between high and low simply by listening to the piano or any other musical instrument. They will also be able to respond bodily.

This analogy can be carried further once they have mastered these concepts. You might ask them to show you where a middle sound might be on their bodies—their waists. They will also develop an understanding of direction—what is going up and coming down, or in musical terms, what is ascending and descending.

Perhaps you have always thought of music instruction as sitting still in a choir rehearsal and singing clear tones, or sitting erect on the piano bench and playing Hanon's finger studies at a phenomenal speed. If so, you have eliminated young children, who are not capable of this type of discipline or muscular coordination.

This is unfair! Many times these same children can achieve exceptional rhythmic precision or are able to learn staff reading quickly. Our definition of *musical* has been too small. In our attempt to define its uniqueness, we have made it far too exclusive. Music has been accessible only to a select few. What a tragedy! If music is a language—and indeed it is—it needs to be universal, both in experience and expression.

So throw your dusty definitions in the closet. Let your imagination expand. Clap to a rousing rhythm, stamp to a grandoise march, and stretch your hands to reach for a high note—music is for everyone!

ICING OR CAKE?

I LOVE BIRTHDAY PARTIES, all kinds—pajama parties, scavenger hunts, a day at the fair—and for any age—youngster, teenager, or grandmother. But my favorites are parties for one-, two-, and three-year-old children.

Invariably the precious toddler and a few of his friends sit down to a table set with all the decorations—favors, hats, paper plates, napkins, and other paraphernalia mom has found at the local store.

With the birthday cake an inch beyond the child's reach and "Happy Birthday" ringing through the air, mom or dad snaps a picture to immortalize the occasion. One minute later the birthday cake and ice cream are distributed, and the fun begins! Quickly the guest of honor delves into the ice cream and frosting, smearing it all over his or her face, chair, place-setting, and anything within a twelve-inch radius. In an attempt to maintain some sort of aesthetic, mom tries to clean up the mess as she advises, "Honey, don't just eat the icing. Eat the cake."

Lots of frosting—thick and gooey—seems to go with kids. The chore is to get them to eat the cake. And yet, parents everywhere instruct their children to eat the cake as well. Why?

Cake is the essence; icing the nonessential extra used to enhance it. Have you ever watched a school board evaluate curriculum? The three basics—reading, writing, and arithmetic—are the essence, the stuff of which education is made. Then come the related and semirelated fields of social studies and the sciences. On a little lower level are such courses as home economics and manual arts. Last on the ladder are the fine arts—music, painting, drama, design. Whenever budget cuts are necessary, guess which program goes first?

And what about the value of music to the church? Is it part of the cake, or just icing? To many church members, music is a vital part of praise and worship. And others who were never reached by dynamic sermons or evangelistic messages are touched by a beautiful hymn or cantata. For many of us, the songs we sing in church or learn in Sunday school become so much a part of us that their message often sustains us in times of trouble.

From a practical standpoint, music education for young church members is worthwhile—not only so they can worship more effectively but also so they can share a gift they might have with others. How often have you heard a good voice in church, but when you suggested that this person sing in the choir, the response was, "I can't. I don't know how to read music." This man or woman might have participated in a children's choir as a child, but was never taught to read music, so his or her voice is lost to the adult choir.

If secular schools do abandon music education, the church may be forced to enlarge its concept of choir and Sunday school music. Already such education in the schools is often cursory.

PART OF THE CAKE

Music is undeniably part of the educational cake, and a tasty part at that. Have you ever watched a child learn the alphabet? One of the most common methods for today's toddlers is to watch "Sesame Street." For an hour in the morning and another in the afternoon, two-year-old Tommy sits in front of the TV, totally captivated by puppets, people, and characters. The alphabet is sung, spoken, and displayed in just about every way imaginable. Before long, Tommy is repeating the alphabet right along with the characters and singing at a volume that lets you know he isn't the shy guy he sometimes pretends to be.

One day you and Tommy pass a K Mart. Excitedly, he points to the sign and cries, "Look, mom. See the K!" You are elated and quickly compliment him. A few months later, Tommy is scribbling on a piece of paper and attempts to draw some lines in a specific order. He thrusts the paper at you and says, "Look, mom. I've made an e." Again you compliment him on how well he knows his alphabet.

What does this process show us about learning? Children like Tommy are experiencing the alphabet by singing songs and speaking words that attract them. Through a variety of repetitive methods, these concepts are internalized until these children can recognize and reproduce the letters by themselves.

Their learning process is complete, because it occurs in three different areas—intellectual, emotional, and physical (or in technical terms, in the cognitive, affective, and psychomotor domains). Tommy's cognitive learning was completed when he recognized the letter on the K Mart sign. But he knew this letter because he first became involved on the affective level—associating with the program emotionally and singing along. Finally this learning was translated into a psychomotor activity when he tried to write an e.

In order for learning to be achieved, all three domains must be involved. If one domain is omitted or deficient, learning is reduced. "Sesame Street" shows how music can link all three domains together, for music does not only affect all three levels; it can also involve all three simultaneously.

One example of this is a game I play with the youngest children called Copycat. As the children imitate me, I touch my head, my ankles, and stretch my hands out to the side. Then I give one quick clap. Their responding claps are staggered. After a pause, I clap again with the same response—each child clapping as he feels like it.

Then I clap twice. The response improves—it is closer to being all together. Next I clap three times and rest. The imitated response again shows improvement. By the third or fourth time of clap, clap, clap, rest, the children invariably clap in unison.

The next week we repeat the game with rhythm instruments. And the following week we might stomp our feet. By the third or fourth week, I might extend this psychomotor activity to the cognitive level.

"Would you like to see the rhythm we are clapping?" I ask. Without any further explanation, I draw three quarter notes and a quarter rest on the blackboard. I may not even mention that they are quarter notes. But as I draw them, I say, "Clap, clap, clap, rest," or "Stomp, stomp, stomp, rest."

Then I ask them to clap or stomp this rhythm while I point to the notes on the board. Now the children begin to visualize the rhythm they have been experiencing emotionally and physically for several weeks.

Later in the class I might have them draw three circles, color them in, and add three stems. This makes a quarter note. As I go around to compliment them on their quarter notes, I add the quarter rest. After a few hours of this kind of fun, a child can clap the rhythm, read it from the board, and write what he has experienced.

And this is not the extent of the music fundamentals a young child can learn. Rhythmic dictation—or the process of writing down a rhythm that is heard—has been limited to college and conservatory music majors. I have found that young children achieve it almost naturally.

GETTING INSIDE

The point of all this is far greater than simply teaching children about squiggles on staff lines. Music's ability to integrate can be applied to virtually every subject in the curriculum. I remember studying Mexico in social studies. We did quite a bit of reading and accumulated a large number of facts, all of which were intriguing. However, when it came time to get a feel for the culture, we were introduced to some Mexican music—especially as it related to the country's customs. Immediately we internalized this culture, not through factual accumulation but through sound.

In the Sunday school situation, a song that describes a biblical event can be sung to increase the student's familiarity with the story and increase retention. Or if the teacher is trying to portray a biblical truth, this can be internalized by singing a song that reveals this truth.

Were you ever involved in a Sunday school contest where you got a prize for learning all the books of the Bible? If you learned them as a young child, you probably learned them to music. Then when you got older and needed to find a certain reference, you had to sing through the song until you got to the correct book.

Or have you ever tried to learn a Scripture passage and almost given up when someone put the words to music? All of a sudden, the difficulty vanished, and you not only memorized the verse, you found yourself singing it throughout the week.

Last summer I worked in several backyard Bible clubs. The theme of our lessons was "Accepting God's Gifts," especially God's gift of creation. I wanted the children to remember the Bible stories we discussed and to experience the joy of God's world.

So instead of using the music that was suggested, which did not relate to our theme, I selected songs that expressed the truths of creation—"All Things Bright and Beautiful," "This Is My Father's World," "This Is the Day the Lord Hath Made" and "It's a Miracle." This music was not only enjoyable, it gave the youngsters an opportunity to internalize the truths they were learning.

Such songs have popped into my mind long after the class period has ended.

One such instance occurred when my husband and I were traveling from Chicago to San Francisco on Interstate 80. We had eaten lunch in Laramie, Wyoming, and were ready to take on the mountain driving after being refreshed. About ten miles out of Laramie, we entered some of the most desolate country I have ever seen. Suddenly the highway was covered with packed snow and ice, the guardrails disappeared, and so did all the other cars.

We were afraid to slow down, because we needed momentum to make the inclines. And we were afraid to go too fast, lest we lose control and catapult into one of the ravines. I became so frightened I couldn't speak.

I don't remember how far we drove that way, but it seemed endless. I wanted to say something to ease the tension, but the words would not come. Finally I remembered a song I had heard as a child, "Tenderly He Watches Over You, Every Step, Every Mile of the Way."

The relief was overwhelming! I knew we would make it. I had memorized plenty of Scripture in my life and knew all kinds of logical arguments. But it was the music—retained in my mind from early childhood—that overcame my fear.

I have heard others relate this same type of experience. Once Dr. Howard Hendricks, a speaker at the Mount Hermon Christian Conference center in California, related how he had let his daughter attend a large secular university—trusting her scriptural training to supply a foundation for her to interact with opposing views. But surprisingly, all the theology and doctrine seemed inadequate. It was the hymns she had learned during childhood that proved to be the foundation on which she could lean.

Music does increase retention. Music can increase motivation. Music involves thinking, emotion, and physical skill. It is not frivolous or irrelevant but substantive and significant. For both churches and schools, music is part of the cake.

"IT'S NOT EASY BEING GREEN"

COME WITH ME for a short tour. I want you to visit several churches. Our tour will include a Sunday school class, children's church, a children's choir rehearsal, and finally a day school music class. Our object will be to observe and be as unobstrusive as possible.

Our first visit will be the primary department of a Sunday school. It's an ordinary Sunday, not a special holiday or season of the year. The teachers have all prepared their lesson on Jonah.

The song leader is not a polished musician, but she loves to sing and knows the children do, too. Since her responsibility is music, she hasn't bothered to read the lesson—it doesn't really have any bearing on what she will do. But she has worked with children in Sunday school for many years and is well acquainted with the songs in the Sunday school repertoire.

Experience has taught her to start with a good, peppy song, so her first choice is "Hallelu, Hallelu, Hallelu, Hallelujah, Praise Ye the Lord." She asks the boys to sing all the "Hallelu's" and the girls all the "Praise Ye the Lord's." Then she will see who sings the loudest.

It isn't long before the room is filled with shouting as the teams try to outdo one another. Any actual worship is lost. But that's okay, the kids are having a good time.

After this, she decides that a change in volume would be a good choice. But she still wants a song that will keep the children involved, like "Deep and Wide."

> Deep and wide, deep and wide,
> There's a fountain flowing deep and wide.
> Deep and wide, deep and wide,
> There's a fountain flowing deep and wide.

The motions are great fun, especially for boys looking for an excuse to "accidentally" bump one another's midsections. As for what the fountain is or why it's flowing . . .

By the time this song is finished, the children are ready to sit down—a remarkable achievement in itself. The leader has reached the first part of her goal—to tire the kids out so they will sit still for the lesson. Next, she needs a song that can be sung sitting down—a lively song that doesn't require any physical exertion. So she suggests the children sing "It's Bubbling."

After prayer time, she gives the children an opportunity to choose one last song before they go to their classes. One eager boy gets his hand up first and requests, "I'm in the Lord's Army." The children cheer as they jump into perfect military position. Their favorite part is when they come to "shoot the artillery." Their machine guns blast away with a vengeance that would make General Patton smile. Finally the opening exercises are concluded, and the children are dismissed to their classes with smiling faces and worn-out bodies.

The next stop on our tour is children's church. The children have been sitting still during their Sunday school lesson, so naturally they need action, and lots of it. A song such as "Father Abraham" fills the need for lots of movement, if nothing else.

The song leader here is young and is comfortable in the youth idiom. One of his favorites has always been "My Lord Knows the Way Through the Wilderness," which is a favorite, since kids love Daniel Boone and Davey Crockett, and a trip through the wilderness sounds like fun.

Finally, the children have an opportunity to select one of their favorites. Someone picks "Give Me Oil in My Lamp, Keep Me Burning." This tune has many varieties—everything from "Make Me Fishers of Men, Keep Me Fishin' " to "Give Me Gas for My Ford, Keep Me Chuggin' in the Lord." By the time everyone is done, they have smiles on their faces, so the young leader decides to capture their mood in song—"If You're Happy and You Know It, Clap Your Hands." Now the song "service" is over. It's time to take the offering and have a missionary story.

A brief lunch and a short drive to the next town brings us to a junior choir rehearsal. The director is a good musician who has worked with the children's choir for about one year. Although she knows kids this age learn quickly by rote, the children have insisted they cannot remember without printed music, so she has given in to them—even though they often hold it upside down.

Still why teach them to read music? Most of them probably won't become professional musicians anyway. Besides, it would bore them—and they have to sing in church in two weeks.

Although they have been working on their music for a few weeks now, each week seems to retrace the same material. Patiently she begins again this day, taking each phrase and teaching it by rote. Then when the children repeat the phrase, she makes any necessary corrections.

After thirty minutes of this tiring process— interrupted every few minutes as she asks the children to please stop talking—she motions for them to stand and go over the entire song. Although their achievement is not commensurate with the amount of time they have spent, she compliments her young singers—knowing that at this point they have been taxed to their limit and need positive reinforcement. Then she quickly moves on to the next song—since they have to perform two—and covers it in a similar manner.

By the end of the rehearsal, the leader is exhausted, and the kids are ready for a good time on the playground. Next week will be dress rehearsal, and the same material will have to be reviewed again for the children who were absent. It seems hard to get past the basics and develop anything really good. But discouragement is allayed by the fact that the kids are getting an opportunity to sing, and involvement is fun.

Our day has been exhausting. But a good night's

sleep and a hearty breakfast should revive us for the final stop on our tour. We're scheduled to observe an elementary music class in a private Christian day school. Here music is once a week for thirty minutes.

We are welcomed by the teacher, in spite of the fact that we wanted to remain unnoticed. The children's excitement shows that this time is eagerly awaited. The music teacher asks two boys to pass out the singing books. Without waiting for the teacher to ask for requests, the children begin raising their hands.

"Can we sing 'Billy Boy' or 'His Banner Over Me'?"

"Can we sing 'There Was a Wise Old King'?" It is apparent that these children have quite a repertoire.

After several minutes of old favorites, the teacher begins to teach a few new songs. She asks them to turn to "Fiddle-dee-dee, Fiddle-dee-dee, the Fly Has Married the Bumblebee." This is a fun song, and the children catch on quickly. Then on through the book to a hymn—this time, one of the most beautiful in our heritage, "For the Beauty of the Earth." This is a bit more challenging, and the children hold their books close to their faces, even though most of them can't read music.

After several attempts at learning this hymn, music time is almost over. The teacher, knowing that it is best to end with a familiar song, quickly closes with a rousing round of "Pop! Goes the Weasel."

Song titles may vary from one area of the country to the next or from one denomination to another, but the basic pattern of our tour prevails. Smiling faces and worn-out bodies are all too often the goal.

SOMETHING BETTER

To form a new concept of music for children, let's

turn again to "Sesame Street." Its teaching techniques, pacing, and creativity are nothing short of genius, embodying much more than first meets the eye. Sit down with paper and pencil and note everything you see on this program for a week. You will find that "Sesame Street" teaches much more than the alphabet and numbers. Values, human relationships, self-esteem, communication, and much more are considered. The show's pacing is marvelous—who would believe a child could sit still that long?

Now examine the music. How does it compare with the sessions we have just observed? Are most of the songs only nonsense or fun? Or do they relate to a child's development?

For years, one of my favorites has been "It's Not Easy Being Green."

It's not that easy bein' green
Having to spend each day the color of the leaves
When I think it could be nicer being red or yellow or gold
Or something much more colorful like that.

It's not that easy bein' green.
It seems you blend in with so many other ordinary things
And people tend to pass you over
'Cause you're not standing out like flashy sparkles in the
    water
Or stars in the sky.

But green's the color of spring
And green can be cool and friendly-like
And green can be big like an ocean or important like a
    mountain
Or tall like a tree.

When green is all there is to be
It could make you wonder why
But why wonder, why wonder

I am green and it will do fine
It's beautiful
And I think it's what I want to be.

That song portrays the human experience of feeling not-okay and resolves it with a statement of self-esteem. Think of the child who is black, or the white youngster who thinks he's better than his Asian friend. The song speaks to both, and even carries a message for adults.

Does that make it out of a child's range? Not at all! The song has value because it is substantive. What's more, its message will stay with children because it is credible. It is not something they will scrap when they get a few years older.

In contrast, look at "Deep and Wide" and "I'm in the Lord's Army." What do they say? Nothing! When children eventually realize their worthlessness, they may close their minds to most church music.

Or take "Give Me Oil in My Lamp, Keep Me Burning." The image here relates to Jesus' parable of the ten virgins, whose lamps were without oil when the bridegroom arrived. But this parable is not familiar to young children and is also likely to be beyond their comprehension. Jesus often talked in parables to delay his listeners' understanding. We can hardly expect children to relate to a little ditty based on a parable that even many adults find perplexing.

Failing to understand the scriptural reference, a child will probably take this image literally.

And what about other songs we heard on our tour? "It's Bubbling in My Soul" gives the child an impression that he has some kind of machine from the "Lawrence Welk Show" located inside him.

This same criticism can be applied to songs that require an understanding of specific imagery. Music that refers to Jesus as the "Rose of Sharon" or the "Lamb of God" needs to be reserved for a time when the child understands these concepts and is also able to move from imagery to reality. This frequently does not occur until the late elementary grades.

Finally, in order to insure credibility, songs must relate to a child's world. I will never forget a program I attended, where a very talented young girl sang a solo that talked about years spent in the bondage of sin. The longer the song continued, the more ridiculous it became. Obviously, this darling nine-year-old hadn't been enslaved by sin for many years—she knew it, and the audience did, too. By the middle of the second chorus, both the girl and the audience were convulsed with laughter. I was glad I could laugh, but I wanted to cry. Why couldn't a song be chosen that related to the child? My mind began to think of all the songs she could have done, and the list was long.

But what about action or fun songs? Doesn't a child need these as well? Indeed he does. But fun songs need to be just that! To confuse them with imagery, worship, or serious meaning is distortion. If you sense the children are needing some exercise, it would be better to make big circles with your arms or march in rhythm or stretch and then relax to music without words than to create a fiasco, which will hurt your credibility in the end.

MUSIC CAN BE RELEVANT

Music does not live in an isolated box. As we discussed earlier, it is part of the learning process. Don't feel that because you are responsible for music in the opening exercises, you shouldn't read the lesson through and select music that relates to it. If you do, you will maximize the learning process and increase retention, giving the child an opportunity to participate in all three domains of learning simultaneously.

Wouldn't it have been delightful if the primary department we visited had opened the day with:

I wonder how it felt to wake up in the belly of a whale
I wonder how it felt to spend the night with Silas in the jail.
I'm just a child, my life is still before me
I just can't wait to see what God has for me
But I know that I will trust Him
And I'll wait to see what life will be for me.

Then the music leader could have talked about what it means to trust someone, relating this to a child's trusting his mommy and daddy to take care of him. A child doesn't spend his morning worrying that mommy won't give him lunch or get him dressed. Jonah did not trust God, and that was why he disobeyed. He ended up in a lot of trouble, because he didn't trust or obey. This truth could then have been expressed musically by singing:

Trust and obey
For there's no other way
To be happy in Jesus
But to trust and obey

If your children's church presentation is on missions, the music should relate to it, tying the entire program together. If your lesson is on creation, why not sing "All Things Bright and Beautiful" instead of "Do, Lord, Oh, Do, Lord, Oh, Do Remember Me."

Music not only contributes to learning, it contributes to worship. Have you examined John 4: 24 recently? Jesus is telling the woman of Samaria about true worship. "God is a Spirit: and they that worship him must worship him in spirit and in truth."

31

What a challenge! True worship is not only entered in truth—or the cognitive domain—but in spirit as well—the affective domain. Since music is part of each, its contribution to worship cannot be overestimated. To deny children the privilege of worship is reducing Sunday school and children's church to the latest fad in children's entertainment.

Although all situations are not conducive to instruction in music fundamentals, graded choir rehearsals and day school classes are naturals. And remember, a song that has been learned cognitively (so that the melodic and rhythmic patterns are understood) as well as affectively has a better chance of retention. Difficult rhythms that have been analyzed and then clapped will be remembered much more accurately than one that has been taught by rote. A choir rehearsal or music class that can incorporate these principles into its fabric will not be scorned as a time filler or a diversion.

What role does music play in your situation? Do you take time to scrutinize the songs you are presenting? Are the texts credible? Do they rely on imagery? Do they relate to a child's world? Perhaps you'll have to throw out 90 percent of your music as worthless. But that's okay. You wouldn't be the first, and let's hope you're not the last. There's plenty of good music around for anyone willing to look a little and apply the basic criteria I have mentioned. Pack some substance into your songs, and they will create the retention and reservoir God intended.

BEYOND I, IV, AND V

TEACHERS, LIKE MOST OTHER professionals, often assume that experience equals skill. A children's worker in the church who has been in his or her position for thirty years is expected to have all the answers, and even all the problems, neatly categorized. What was "good" for children thirty years ago is still "good" today.

But just because it was used then and has managed to survive is no validation of its worth. Many times we excuse our lack of creativity or openness to new ideas by saying, "It was good enough then," when it really wasn't and hasn't improved with age.

Not only are many of us in a rut when it comes to

selection, but many of our songs sound the same. We change a note or two—perhaps alter the rhythm a little—but keep the same basic harmonic structure.

Several years ago an article in *Time* magazine described a city just south of San Francisco—Daly City, usually known for its tremendous fog. But this article discussed its housing. A builder had bought most of the land to erect moderate-sized homes on each lot. Only the basic plan for each home was the same. The fronts were altered to give a fraction of individuality, but from the back each house looked alike.

Today if you drive along the freeway through Daly City or even get off onto some of its side streets, you find yourself in a rut of houses. The overall design isn't bad, the construction quality is fine, and in fact, the market prices are quite high. The only tragedy is the monotony.

THE RUT OF I, IV, AND V

We find the same thing in much of the music we select for children. In addition to the monotony, the rationale restricting children's music to a simple melody or harmony is ill-founded. Because the child's ear is so receptive to sounds and absorbs them so quickly, while the ear of an adult is already fixed, children are more capable of some complexities in music than most adults. In order for an adult to reproduce a complex rhythm, intellectual analysis is required, while a child will absorb it into the ear and reproduce it almost without thinking.

I'll never forget the expression on a group of mothers' faces when I introduced a new song in class one day. It was undoubtedly the wordiest song with the most intricate rhythm and most complex melody of any I had

34

ever taught to children. I could tell by the mothers' expressions that inside they were saying, *These kids can't possibly do that! Why, we couldn't do it if we tried.*

The song was highly syncopated, the melody non-repetitive, and the words all multisyllable. Yet the kids loved it! The mothers stared in astonishment as the children handled it with ease and enjoyment.

The problem comes when we forget the natural music ability of children and impose upon them a rut of simple harmonies, melodies, and rhythms. Most leaders look for songs that have a ¾ or 4/4 rhythm, many repeated notes, and nothing more than the three primary chords—I, IV, and V. While this may be a satisfactory skeletal structure, keeping children at this level sells their ability short and fosters severe musical deficiencies.

While it is important to keep a child's vocal range in mind, it is equally important to realize that repeated notes are more difficult to sing than some intervals and diatonic passages. And songs with melodic interest are easier to learn. Songs that have melodic, harmonic, and rhythmic variety will beckon the child into a learning experience.

A perfect example is the theme from "Sesame Street." It has rather complex intervals and syncopated rhythms; yet most two-year-olds can sing it with extraordinary precision.

Unfortunately, the church has taken simple chords and made them the center and circumference of its harmonic structure—especially in children's music, but also in most gospel music.

I am not suggesting that all songs have complex texts, intricate melodies, complicated rhythms, and involved harmonic structure. But one or two of these would be advisable if we are to build a credible experience. When a song does not possess any of these characteristics, its value should be questioned. Many songs that have been around for years should be reexamined in the light of these principles. Some would pass the test. Others would be recognized for what they really are.

Do not worry that this approach would catapult you into the use of Bach chorales and German hymns only. Hopefully it will challenge you to include hymn singing, but it should also include the other end of the spectrum. How is this possible?

A VARIETY OF IDIOM

Imagine that in your Christian education department, Sunday school, or children's church you are studying a unit on God's love. The children could memorize Romans 5: 8, "But God commendeth his love toward us, in that, while we were yet sinners, Christ died for us." Possibilities for musical expression of this truth range from the hymn "And Can It Be":

Amazing love
How can it be
That Thou my God
Should'st die for me

to the beautiful new chorus "Oh, How He Loves You and Me."

Oh, how he loves you and me
Oh, how he loves you and me
He gave his life
What more could he give?
Oh, how he loves you
Oh, how he loves me
Oh, how he loves you and me.

Perhaps you are studying the periods of religious persecution in a school history class, and you need an activity to express what the class has learned. Why not sing "Faith of Our Fathers"?

> Faith of our fathers, living still
> In spite of dungeon, fire, and sword
> Oh, how our hearts beat high with joy
> Whene'er we hear that glorious word.
> Faith of our fathers, holy faith!
> We will be true to thee till death.

What about the kindergarten class that is learning about the uniqueness of each individual God made? Educators call it self-esteem. Try teaching the Gaither tune "I Am a Promise."

> I am a promise, I am a possibility
> I am a promise, with a capital "P"
> I am a great big bundle of potentiality.
> And I am learning to hear God's voice
> And I am trying to make the right choices,
> I'm a promise to be anything God wants me to be.

None of these songs is from Handel's *Messiah*. Yet a wide diversity of idiom is exemplified. The hymn "And Can It Be" is one of the great hymns of the church. Although rhythmically simple—meaning that it uses quarter and half notes and regular divisions of the beat—the melody continues to build throughout the song. "Oh, How He Loves You and Me" repeats the same words and has a singable melody, but the lush harmony provides a beautiful structure on which the melody can rest. "Faith of Our Fathers" does not have complex rhythm or harmony, but the words convey a significant message. And "I Am a Promise" provides the kind of charm mentioned earlier in the chapter—a fascinating wordiness combined with syncopated rhythm and a few secondary chords.

The spectrum is wide! Don't feel tied down. You have just been set free from the meaningless jingles perpetuated over the years, from the limitations of one phrase repeated again and again, from melodic and harmonic monotony, and rhythmic simplicity. No longer will you have to interest children in something that has bored you. Your selections should not be limited to the funny little music with tiny-tot titles. The possibilities are unlimited—not only in text but in harmony, melody, and rhythm as well.

A SENSE OF DIRECTION

ANYONE WHO'S EATEN in a college cafeteria for very long knows what happens every few weeks, when leftovers accumulate to a certain point. On such evenings, wise students opt for McDonald's, while the unwary find themselves face-to-face with a curious entree. At the school I attended it was called "shepherd's pie"—everything from the past weeks cooked in a pan with a small amount of gravy, and topped with whipped potatoes that were baked to a golden brown.

The topping looked delicious, but the inside was a potpourri of every kind of vegetable and ground-up stuff imaginable. I hated it!

Many services, Sunday school classes, children's church programs, and music classes have the same sort of catastrophic conglomeration. And many so-called rallies are nothing more than a variety show—each musical group or soloist trying to outdo the other with no continuity. The effect may be entertaining, but it hardly enlarges one's perspective of spiritual truth.

Not that there's anything wrong with entertainment. I love musical variety shows. But most of us don't go to church to be entertained.

Even within the context of a Christian school, music can have a greater part in the learning process if its repertoire and involvement are cohesively woven together. To bounce from "Fiddle-dee-dee" to "For the Beauty of the Earth" to "Pop! Goes the Weasel" lacks impact and reduces music to a time filler or diversion. Yet we constantly find such hodgepodges.

How can they be avoided? The answer is really not difficult. We need to organize our music into carefully designed units, observing principles of direction and good programming.

What if schoolteachers did not determine that children should be able to read and do simple addition and subtraction by a certain point in their education? Our schools would obviously become a jumble of disjoined activities. Because educators have designed careful steps to achieve their goals, education is linear. If we would chart out goals for specific songs to be part of children's repertoire by the time they reached a certain age, we would find ourselves with such a lineup that we would have no time for meaningless jingles.

ESTABLISHING GUIDELINES

After a goal is set, how does one go about charting a

logical course of progression? Again, the answer is not complicated. A good starting place is to coordinate your music with the direction of your curriculum—whether it be science or social studies, Sunday school or children's church. If you are doing a unit on creation, let this be the thread that weaves the Bible lesson, Scripture memorization, and music participation together. The possibilities are unlimited.

And now that you have a guideline, you can put all the principles of selection to work. "All Things Bright and Beautiful," "This Is My Father's World," "This Is the Day the Lord Hath Made," and "God Made Everything" are only a few suggestions.

Perhaps your staff has decided to build a program around praise. Why not take the verse "I will bless the Lord at all times: his praise shall continually be in my mouth" (Ps. 34:1) and have this be the thread? Music can range from "Praise Him, Praise Him, All Ye Little Children" to the "Doxology" to "May Jesus Christ Be Praised" or the little chorus "Praise Him, Praise Him."

If the task seems gargantuan, don't be discouraged. An abrupt change is not the most desirable approach. But a gradual turn, carried out with precision, can put you on the right track faster than you can imagine.

You may have to eliminate the children's opportunity to select a song for several weeks, since their reservoir of music needs to be changed. However, if you design other ways of creative participation and display enthusiasm, the children will reflect your attitude and be won over.

Another key to success is to have the leaders who work with toddlers and preschoolers understand these concepts. Some songs should be introduced into a child's experience at the earliest ages. If the leader is not a polished musician, good records will be an excel-

41

lent substitute. Children love to sing to them, and they allow kids to be part of a successful ensemble. Remember, success breeds motivation.

A child who has learned "All Things Bright and Beautiful" and "God Made Everything" in the preschool department is ready for "This Is My Father's World" and "This Is the Day that the Lord Hath Made" in the primary department. The next building block could be made in grades three and four with "For The Beauty of the Earth" and "I Sing the Mighty Power of God."

Can you see the potential of this approach? Not only can we be assured that by the time a child finishes elementary school he knows the story of Adam and Eve and how God made the stars and the Garden of Eden, but he understands the doctrine of creation as it relates to his world today! He has internalized this truth. It is part of his daily experience. This is *mastery*—mastery on all three levels—cognitive, affective, and psychomotor.

And this is only one doctrine. The same potential exists for all foundational truths.

When God promised, "Train up a child in the way he should go: and when he is old, he will not depart from it" (Prov. 22: 6), he did not endorse haphazard teaching. "The way he should go" is the direction we've been talking about. The course is to be set as a child. To postpone the training until later life negates the prerequisite for the promise.

If music can affect that training, if music can help construct that way, if music can aid in actualizing learning and increasing retention, then music should be governed by the same direction that determines any course of instruction. If we do our part to fulfill God's prerequisite, we are entitled to his promise.

42

A SOLUTION TO THE WIGGLES

IT WAS A WEEKDAY EVENING this past winter. I was in the kitchen preparing dinner for the family, and Stephen was keeping me company by playing there—most of the time under my feet. He had brought a handful of his Fisher-Price people up from his room and was talking with them as only a two-year-old can talk to a doll.

He carefully arranged them in a lopsided circle. Then he stood up and began to circle around them singing, "Ring around the rosey / Pocket full of posies / Ashes, ashes / We all fall down." He fell down so that his carefully erected circle was completely destroyed, and he had to begin the process all over again. This little game continued for several minutes.

The delight in his voice captured my attention and made me giggle inside as I watched the beauty of a young child's imagination. It didn't make any difference that they weren't real people. They could be involved in his little game just by standing there and letting him go around in circles.

I don't know who invented "Ring Around the Rosey." But I do know that it is one of the first games a child learns and seems to be transcultural, for many cultures have their own version or modification.

If you carefully analyze the song's melodic pattern, you will note that it is comprised mostly of a descending minor third—the most natural interval for young children to sing. There's little doubt that the fun part is "we all fall down." For some strange reason, children love to fall down, especially when it is planned. However, I think the charm of this song is much simpler than that. It is a game, and children love games.

I walked into a very difficult teaching situation several months ago. I had come to a Christian elementary school in the middle of the year to follow a teacher whom the children loved. I was naturally the scapegoat for their disappointment over Mrs. Jones's leaving. I became even more unpopular when I informed them we would be learning some music fundamentals— although I didn't use this terminology.

After several weeks of trying to win their confidence and teach them something as well, I watched one day as a class of fifth-graders came in with a nonchalant attitude that seemed almost impenetrable. Finally, when everyone was seated, I announced, "Today we are going to have a relay race."

"You mean a regular relay race, outside and everything?" they replied.

"No," I explained, "but it will be a relay race. This is the way it works. I have two stacks of cards at the front of the room. Beside each stack is an answer sheet. When I say 'Go,' the first person on each side is to run up and look at the first card. Decide what the name of the note is, write your answer on the sheet of paper, and run back and tap the next person in line."

The enthusiasm mounted as the teams prepared to race. Suddenly music fundamentals had become fun. It was the same material we had been working on for several weeks—the names of the lines and spaces of the staff. But now we were using a game. For weeks afterward, the class's attitude was one of anticipation rather than apathy. What game would we do next? they wondered. My creativity was challenged!

THEORY GAMES

Another time I used games effectively was when I was leading a primary choir in San Francisco a couple of years ago. The children were typical of many first-, second-, and third-graders: the boys rowdy, the girls more anxious to learn. We would spend a few minutes on staff reading, and then I would have all the children line up on the carpet.

Before they had come in, I had placed five lines of masking tape on the floor. Then I had added a treble clef out of tape and a dotted line to identify the location of middle C. When I asked the children to line up, I had them stand so their toes just touched the middle-C line. When I called the name of a note, they had to move quickly to that note's location on the staff.

"E—one, two, three, four, five, six, seven, eight, nine, ten, stop!" I would yell as fast as possible. When I got to "Stop!" the children had to freeze wherever they were. Children who were on the first line of the treble clef or in the top space—the two locations for E—were allowed to remain standing. The others had to be seated. It was exciting to see how quickly they learned the names of the lines and spaces.

Another teaching game I use is to pass around a stack of flash cards with one note on each card. I distribute them so every child has one card, except one who is "it" and sits in the middle of the circle. He then points to a child. If this child can identify the note on his or her own card, the youngster in the middle must choose someone else . . . and so on, until the child in the center finds someone who can't. If "it" can correctly identify this child's note, they exchange places and the other child becomes "it."

Last fall I was trying to teach the verse "For he shall give his angels charge over thee, to keep thee in all thy ways" (Ps. 91:11) to my primary choir. After having them repeat it several times with me, I passed out one blue card to each child, face down. I told them that each card had one word of the verse on it. When I said "Go," they were to see how quickly they could arrange themselves in the proper order. The experience was delightful! All of a sudden I had a dozen teachers, all quoting the verse and saying it to one another as they endeavored to unscramble their cards.

PRESCHOOL GAMES

Because preschoolers love to copy one another, Copycat or Mr. Echo is a fun game for them. I have walked into many situations where the children would not sing when I asked them to. So I have begun by saying, "Let's play a game!" I would ask them to be my echo, and then I would sing, "How are you?"

The children would repeat, "How are you?"
Then I would sing, "I am fine."
And again they would echo, "I am fine."
This simple game may not impress you at first. But analyze its learning process. The approach is being made through the ear—the most natural way to enter a young child's experience. He hears and imitates the melodic sequence.

At a previous point in the lesson—perhaps during the rhythmic activity—the children may have clapped to the rhythm (quarter note, quarter note, quarter note, rest). Now I'm employing the same rhythmic pattern in a completely different approach—melodic imitation. This type of correlation equips the child with another physical expression of the rhythm he has mastered. And this time, it is coupled with a tune.

The third dimension is to place the notes on the staff as we sing. Since the children are comfortable with the melodic imitation, this, too, is well within their grasp. When they master this skill, they will be able to read the melodic sequence from the chalkboard, understand the melody and the rhythm, and express it vocally. This demonstrates a mastery of eye-ear-vocal coordination—a sophisticated achievement for any student. The game approach did it all.

GAMES INVOLVING ALL DIMENSIONS

Games can also be used to involve the student in all three dimensions of learning. One of my classes had spent several weeks in rhythm activities built around four basic patterns. The children could imitate them when I clapped, stomped, snapped my fingers, spoke them, and played them on a rhythm instrument. We had also practiced rhythm reading—looking at a rhythmic pattern in their books or on the chalkboard and reading it verbally as we pointed to the notes. Now I wanted to bring the two experiences together so they could read a rhythmic pattern and perform it.

Before class I had written the various patterns on individual cards and had hidden them around the room. When the children came in, I told them that we were going to play a special game of hide-and-seek. I would play a certain rhythm on an instrument, and they had to look around the classroom until they found the secret message with that rhythm on it. When they found it, they were to bring it to me and share their treasure with the rest of the class. In order to achieve this goal, a child had to hear a rhythm internally to be sure it matched what he was hearing from me, read it on the card, and perform it—the psychomotor development that is so essential to mastery.

TEAM GAMES

Team games can also be fun. For instance, the flash card game described earlier can be used as a team endeavor. These cards might have a rhythmic pattern, a specific note, a musical symbol, or a melodic pattern written on them. As long as the team members give correct answers, their team can continue—hoping to get all the way through their line without missing an answer. If they miss, the turn passes to the opposing team, and they continue to answer until they miss.

Group activities of this nature allow all members of a team to share in the success. Many times a student's motivation is destroyed because someone else always gets the right answer or finishes just a split second before him or her. Team success spreads the joy around. In the same manner, defeat in a team situation takes the personal failure out, which may result in group determination to win the next time rather than discouragement and an unwillingness to try.

GAMES WITHOUT A LOSER

Games can also be structured so there are no winners or losers. Circle games are often this way; no one is in front or leading the march, and everyone is the same. I remember teaching a group of four-year-olds. Most of the children were somewhat reluctant to leave their mothers and join my circle. So I invited the moms to join me, and if their child wanted to come along, okay.

Then I began clapping a steady beat. The moms joined in immediately. One by one the children did, too. Then I tapped my right foot in the same beat, then my left, then snapped my fingers, and tapped my shoulders and the end of my nose—until everyone was participating.

When I began the same process all over again, I assigned a definite pattern to the procedure, rather than just a steady beat. After the pattern was well established and perpetuating itself on group momentum, I went to the piano and began to sing, "I clap, clap, clap, and stamp, stamp, and turn myself around. . . ."

My game needed no instruction to be a success. Before long we were clapping, stamping, touching the floor, and snapping our fingers in unison. We circled to the right, then to the left, turned around, and stretched up high. The children were amazed that music class could be so much fun! And games that are fun will undoubtedly be taken home, where they will be taught to dolls, parents, siblings, friends, and relatives.

I have found that games are a great way to involve children in the learning process. They require active participation—not sleepy minds—and they give the child an opportunity to dominate the activity, which is usually the teacher's privilege. They stimulate action—a perfect solution for all the wiggles that need an outlet. And they spark group momentum, a much stronger force than teacher motivation. Quite often they can spread the delight of success to many who might not achieve it otherwise.

CREATIVITY UNDER CONSTRUCTION

WHEN I WAS EIGHT, my parents decided to build a cottage on Cape Cod. There were no grandiose plans for it to be a second home by the ocean, but rather a tiny bungalow—fourteen by twenty-four feet—where we could retreat from the hectic pace of a pastor's home and relax in the quiet surroundings of nature.

One reason I remember building this cottage is that my parents took time to be creative and involve our family. When some branches needed to be cut from several trees, the man who drove the bulldozer suggested that he lift my brother up in the scoop of his machine to do it. My dad taught me how to use a plumb line, and mom taught me to nail up clapboards. All of us had fun, and regardless of its size, this bungalow was our palace when it was finished.

Creativity also gives life to learning. When God made Adam he formed him according to a specific design, but it wasn't until He breathed the breath of life into him that man became a living soul. The formation was scientific; the breath creative.

While it is imperative that learning have a goal and a direction to achieve it, this is not enough. Creativity is needed—that breath of life, that individual aspect that distinguishes it from assembly-line thinking.

Maybe your goal is staff reading. Before you start, be sure the children understand the difference between on-a-line and in-a-space. Learn only a few notes at a time so that success is built in. Then use flash cards, relay races, masking tape lines on the floor, a bean bag toss, writing games, and anything else you can think of. Sing your melodies by note names. Write segments of the melodies you sing. But make staff reading more than E-G-B-D-F.

Maybe your goal is to achieve a difficult rhythmic passage. Start out with imitation. Use a handclap or a finger snap. Add a rhythm instrument. Maybe you will want to intone some words to the rhythm. Write it on the board. Have the children write it on paper. Then have them find it in a piece of music. Or have it be a secret message that is necessary to enter class next week. There are thousands of possibilities.

PIECING THE PUZZLE TOGETHER

One year I remember teaching "We Praise Thee, O God, Our Redeemer" to a primary choir. I had been working with them only a few weeks, and everything that had been done previously could be categorized as typical. We had a relatively short time to learn the song for a Thanksgiving service presentation. Although I thought the melody was probably familiar—it had the same tune as "We Gather Together"—it was not. The children were having trouble with the words, the melody, the rhythm, and finally in putting the entire song together.

I had begun to teach staff reading the first time we met. The children caught on quickly and within a few weeks knew from bass clef C to treble clef C. We had used many of the games already mentioned. It was time to put their skill to work. One at a time I put the notes on the board and had them read them—G-G-A-G-E-F-G-F-E-D-E-C, etc. I wrote enough notes to cover the first musical phrase. We talked about the melody—when the notes stayed the same, when they went up, and when they went down. Then we sang the melody by note name. It fit together beautifully.

This game turned the corner for us. The melody had been brought within their reach. They sang the tune as though they had known it all their lives. The parents who were assisting me were amazed. How could these children have achieved such a difficult task—learning the melody to a hymn by reading it by note name and then singing it in the same manner? But the foundation had been laid. The basic structure was there. I had begun with a goal in mind and direction to achieve that goal. Then creativity had given it life.

But the words still posed a similar problem.

We praise Thee, O God, our Redeemer, Creator
In grateful devotion our tribute we bring;
We lay it before Thee, we kneel and adore Thee,
We bless thy holy name, glad praises we sing.

Out came Mr. Echo. I would say one line, and the

children would repeat it. But I did not use a monotone voice. One time I would say it *piano,* or softly, and ask the children to repeat it in a *piano* voice. The next time I would make it *mezzo piano,* or medium soft, and ask them to do the same. Gradually I would increase my voice, until we reached *forte,* or loud. Then we diminished in the same manner.

This treatment not only added interest but also provided an opportunity for the children to experience dynamic control, dynamic markings, and progression from one volume to the next. I would return to these concepts later when I put the entire song together and wanted some phrases louder or softer than others.

For now I divided the group into four teams. Each team was assigned one line. I could point to any team at any time and in any order. Then it was their job to say the words before I counted to ten. Another possibility would have been to return to a game I mentioned earlier—writing individual lines on cards and having the children combine these lines to form the verse.

We approached the rhythm to this song in a similar manner. We had been imitating it, clapping and marching to it, reading and writing it. When we put the melody, the words, and the rhythm together, each part related to their previous experience. Although the children hadn't realized it, I had been piecing together a puzzle. Now I saw their faces visually communicate. *Oh, that was the rhythm we marched to last week,* or *Hey, those are the words we just played that game with,* or *That's the same melody we have been singing in letter names for three weeks.* The response was gratifying.

I remember another time I was particularly impressed with the benefits of teaching music fundamentals this way. One day I was observing a class of children I had taught the year before. The rhythm activity for that hour consisted of a game similar to "Simon Says." The teacher had made up cards with one measure of a four-measure rhythm missing, and the children had to fill in the appropriate rhythm. The teacher told them how many notes they were allotted, and they had to assign the necessary beats to each note.

I thought the idea was terrific but hard. However, the children pulled it off with greater ease and enthusiasm than I could have imagined. Why? Again, the foundation had been laid. We had spent the previous year experiencing quarter notes, half notes, whole notes, dotted notes, and eighth notes. The goal had been set: to make these children rhythmically independent— capable of reading any rhythmic combination of these notes. The direction had been logical—we had progressed from the most simple to the more complex, with much repetition. We had involved every aspect of the learning process. And then creativity had given it life!

Music is a language—a language that transcends culture, a language for everybody, a language that breaks down the traditional patterns of achievement for the older and more mature and distributes them among the very young.

And music is essential. It holds its place at the very core of the education process. It is not frivolous or irrelevant but substantive enough that it affects our intellect, our emotions, and our physical reactions, sometimes simultaneously. And it is active—not passive. It defies the cobwebs of stoic education and says, "Come, get involved—participate in many different ways." It beckons with a charm and intrigue that is obvious, but can't be captured and put into a neatly wrapped package.

MUSIC IS FOR CHILDREN

Music can convey truth, express feelings, develop social poise, and establish self-esteem through the texts it employs. None of God's other gifts has such an ability to penetrate the entire person.

Certainly a gift of this magnitude (and we have only scratched the surface) must be reserved for royalty, the elite, the intelligentsia? No, the remarkable thing is that music is not reserved for anyone. Music is for everyone—most of all, music is for children!

Appendixes

ABOUT THE AUTHOR

Connie Fortunato is director of Christian education and a graded choir program at Bethel Church in San Jose, California. She has written several songs for children and is writing a graded choir curriculum for David C. Cook Publishing Co.

Her approach to music for children is based on experience as a teacher of music at Baymonte Christian School in Scotts Valley, California, and as an initiator of the Yamaha music schools for preschoolers in Wheaton, Illinois, and Hayward, California.

Mrs. Fortunato is a graduate of Wheaton College with a major in music, and a veteran of a Youth For Christ overseas musical group. Her husband, Jim, is chairman of the music department of Bethany Bible College in Santa Cruz. They have two young children, Stephanie and Stephen.

A WORKSHOP IDEA

From the  IDEABANK

PREPARATION

1. Get a "Sesame Street" record or tape of the song "It's Not Easy Being Green."

2. Copy the words to this song on a ditto or chart so the participants can read them. (See the text of this session for the lyrics.)

3. Set up a display table of:
- the songbooks and hymnals used in your church
- a few secular songbooks for children (such as the Walt Disney songbook)
- a book of folk songs (such as *The Fireside Book of Folksongs*)
- Christian and a few secular record albums for children (A local Christian bookstore and a music store might be willing to lend you albums for display.)
- If your church has a children's choir, you might include some copies of their music.
- If you are using a choir curriculum, you might display a copy of the student's and teacher's books and some of the teaching aids.

4. Give the teachers an opportunity to browse while you play an album of children's music, preferably one that uses a children's choir or ensemble.

MEETING PLAN

THE IMPORTANCE OF MUSIC

Begin the session by asking why music is important to the church. Here are some thoughts you might wish to include:
- Music is a vital part of praise and worship.
- Music can sometimes reach people who are not touched by a sermon or evangelistic message.
- Songs and hymns can sustain us in times of difficulty.
- Music can reinforce curriculum.

Go into the last statement more specifically. You might suggest that music is not a frill or time filler in the church's ministry to children but an essential part of the learning process. Children often learn the alphabet easier as a song. The same is true for the books of the Bible or a verse of Scripture.

But for the Christian, music is even more central. In many ways, music is the Christian faith's most natural language. Even the psalmist couldn't separate the two. Worship is a song of the spirit—sometimes using words, sometimes not.

A GOOD CHILDREN'S SONG

Suggest that since music is an important part of a child's spiritual growth, more consideration should be given to the songs that are selected. Then explain that you are going to consider the elements of a good children's song.

Use the secular song "It's Not Easy Being Green," one that is extremely popular with children and used as an example by Connie Fortunato in this book.

Play this song as the teachers follow the words.

It's not that easy bein' green
Having to spend each day the color of the leaves
When I think it could be nicer being red or yellow or gold
Or something much more colorful like that.

It's not that easy bein' green.
It seems you blend in with so many other ordinary things
And people tend to pass you over
'Cause you're not standing out like flashy sparkles in the water
Or stars in the sky.

But green's the color of spring
And green can be cool and friendly-like
And green can be big like an ocean or important like a mountain
Or tall like a tree.

When green is all there is to be
It could make you wonder why
But why wonder, why wonder
I am green and it will do fine
It's beautiful
And I think it's what I want to be.

Then ask them to identify the qualities that make this an appeal-

60

ing song. You will want to include:

1. Good melody and rhythm, not just repetitive patterns
2. Imagery that is suited to the child's level—save most songs with imagery until the late elementary grades
3. Words that are relevant to the child's world and have a personal meaning or message
4. Feelings that are important to a child's development

Write these four criteria on your overhead chart or blackboard, explaining that not all these elements will be present in every song, but a song should contain some of them.

Then apply these criteria to the songs you are using in your Christian education program. Ask the teachers to list five or six songs that meet these criteria. Share their choices, writing the ones everyone agrees with on the overhead chart or chalkboard.

SONGS THAT ARE RELEVANT TO YOUR CURRICULUM

If your church school has a song leader, this person could conduct a short discussion session with the teachers to determine songs that could be used in her sessions that are relevant to curriculum. The teachers could share the topics of their upcoming lessons, and the song leader could begin a list of songs she will use.

For instance, if the children are studying a unit on creation, the song leader might choose "All Things Bright and Beautiful," "This Is My Father's World," "This Is the Day the Lord Hath Made," and "It's a Miracle."

This would also be a good time to discuss how the song leader can keep in touch with the monthly lesson plans.

If you church school is divided into age levels—primary, primary-junior, junior, etc.—divide into these groups for this discussion.

ADDITIONAL IDEAS

Here are some other ideas for this period of time:
- If your church has begun a children's choir program, you might have the children's choir director explain this curriculum, showing the teachers some of the new methods and teaching aids.

61

- If you do not use an outside resource person, you might split the teachers into three groups and have them discuss their current lessons plans, how music might add to these lessons, and what songs would be important.

Have them come back together and share some of their ideas.

USING MUSIC IN THE CLASSROOM

Now begin a discussion of effective ways to use music in the classroom. You might suggest the following ideas:

- Using records that apply to what the class is studying. Albums are available:

1. That present Old and New Testament stories—*The Purple Puzzle Tree* (Concordia)

2. That portray spiritual truths—the Gaither albums, such as *Especially for Children* and *Bill Gaither With the Sunday School Picnic;* the Paul Johnson album *Here Come the Kids;* and Annie Herring's *Kids of the Kingdom.*

3. That present a melodic interpretation of a child's spiritual growth—Cam and Cher Floria's *The Enchanted Journey.*

- A Bible story, such as Jonah and the whale, can be supplemented by singing "I Wonder How It Felt."

I wonder how it felt to wake up in the belly of a whale
I wonder how it felt to spend the night with Silas in the jail,
I'm just a child, my life is still before me
I just can't wait to see what God has for me
But I know that I will trust Him
And I'll wait to see what life will be for me.

- To enhance a unit that is built around the concept of praise, a teacher might have the class memorize Psalm 34:1, "I will bless the Lord at all times: his praise shall continually be in my mouth," and sing the following songs: "Praise Him, Praise Him, All Ye Little Children," the "Doxology," "May Jesus Christ Be Praised," and the little chorus "Praise Him, Praise Him."

Emphasize that if a teacher is not comfortable leading a song, the children can sing to records. And stress the importance of continuity. A child who has learned "All Things Bright and Beautiful" and "God Made Everything" in the preschool department is ready for "This Is My Father's World" and "This Is the Day that the

Lord Hath Made" in primary. The next building block could be made in grades three and four with "For the Beauty of the Earth" and "I Sing the Mighty Power of God." It is important to begin music in the preschool years.

TO CLOSE

Stress that we need to approach music in the church thoughtfully, because music is an important part of an adult's and a child's spiritual growth. Reemphasize this point, not from your own experience this time, but from biblical authority.

Music was not added to worship by early church leaders. It is first mentioned in the Bible in Genesis 4 and is part of worship from then on.

Nor is the importance of music merely conjecture. We all know that David soothed Saul by playing the harp.

And it came to pass, when the evil spirit from God was upon Saul, that David took an harp, and played with his hand: so Saul was refreshed, and was well, and the evil spirit departed from him.—1 Samuel 16:23

But the importance of music is also seen in other parts of the Bible. Before Elisha prophesied to the three kings who were attacking Moab, he made the following request:

But now bring me a minstrel. And it came to pass, when the minstrel played, that the hand of the Lord came upon him.—2 Kings 3:15

The psalmist constantly exhorts us to praise God through song. One such example is Psalm 33:2-3:

Praise the Lord with harp: sing unto him with the psaltery and an instrument of ten strings. Sing unto him a new song.

This same "new song" is mentioned in Revelation, where the 24 elders are pictured singing a new song before the throne of God.

It is truly scriptural to say that music is an important part of man's communication with God, both on earth and in heaven.